Natural Resources

by Carol Levine

PEARSON
Scott
Foresman

Parts of Earth

Earth has many things we use. Useful things that come from nature are called **natural resources.** Some natural resources are air, water, and land. Natural resources are important to all living things.

The surface of Earth is made up of land and water. Earth has more water than land. Land with water all around it is an island.

Kinds of Land

There are many kinds of land. Some land is flat. Plains are flat lands. Some land goes up. Hills and mountains go up.

Kinds of Water

There are many kinds of water. Ocean water covers a lot of Earth. Stream water runs on top of land.

Ocean

Stream

Rocks

Rocks are nonliving things. They come from Earth. Rocks are natural resources. Rocks can be different shapes. Rocks can be different sizes. Big rocks are boulders. Small rocks are pebbles. **Sand** is tiny pieces of broken rock.

Rock

Pebbles

Sand

Some living things use rocks. These bats
live in a cave. Their home is made of rock.
These houses were built with rocks.

Soil

Part of Earth's land is soil. Soil is a natural resource.

Different kinds of soil look and feel different. Soil is made of different things. Sand and **clay** can be in soil. Humus can be in soil too. **Humus** is made of parts of things that were once living.

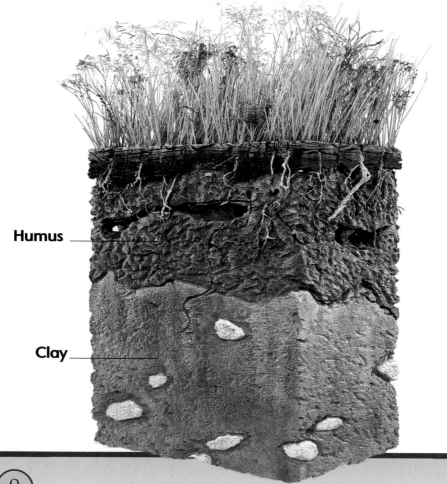

Humus

Clay

Land Changes

Land on Earth changes. Sometimes weathering changes land. **Weathering** is when water and ice break and change rocks. Weathering changes the shape, color, and size of rocks. These sea pebbles took a long time to become smooth.

Sometimes erosion changes Earth. **Erosion** is when wind or water moves rocks and soil. A beach may look different after a big storm. There may be less sand. Erosion makes this change.

Using Natural Resources

Living things use natural resources in different ways.

Air

We do not see air. We can feel air when it blows as wind. People, animals, and plants all need air to live.

Water

Living things use water. Water helps living things. How do you use water?

Land

Land is important too. Food for people can grow in soil. Some plants grow in soil. Many living things live on land.

Graphite

Minerals

Minerals are nonliving things. They are
natural resources in rocks and soil. Graphite
is a mineral people use. It can be used to
make the inside part of pencils.

Saving Natural Resources

Air must be clean. Dirty air is bad for living things. We can help air stay clean. Water and land must be clean too. We all can help. Pick up litter and trash. Use less water when you can.

Ways to Help

There are many ways to save natural resources. You can help!

Reduce means to use less. Reuse means to use again. Recycle means to make old things into new things. What can you do to help reduce, reuse, and recycle?

Glossary

clay   a sticky kind or part of soil

erosion   when wind or water moves rocks and soil

humus   a part of soil that is made of things that were once alive

minerals   nonliving natural resources found in rocks and soil that people use

natural resource a useful thing that comes from nature

rocks   nonliving natural resources that come from Earth

sand   very tiny pieces of broken rock

weathering when water and ice change the size, shape, or color of rocks